This vintage postcard has at least a couple of different "lost" elements. First, notice that it shows no interstate highways crisscrossing the state. Second, it illustrates the Georgia state flag that was adopted at the beginning of the civil rights era in 1956, incorporating the Confederate battle flag. Since 2001, the Georgia flag has been redesigned twice.

Lost Attractions

of

GEORGIA

· TIM HOLLIS

THE
History
PRESS

Published by The History Press
Charleston, SC
www.historypress.com

Cover images: courtesy of the author except *front cover, top center*: Marietta Museum of History collection.

Unless otherwise noted, all images are courtesy of the author.

First published 2021

Manufactured in the United States

ISBN 9781467146937

Library of Congress Control Number: 2020948635

CONTENTS

ACKNOWLEDGEMENTS

Although most of the material you will see in the pages that follow originated in my own decades-long collection of memorabilia, credit must be given to the additional sources that enlivened the result. As you will notice in the credit lines for the photos, a number of them (as well as other helpful information) came from fellow tourism collectors and photographers: Marla Akin, Nelson Boyd, Tim Campbell, Al Coleman, Shaunnon Drake, Andy Duckett, Manuel Fernandez, Bette Justice, David Kelleher, Jeremy Kennedy, Doug Kirby, Rita Martin, Mark Pedro, Amy Reed, Bea Rumley, Katie Sidwell and Russell Wells.

We must also acknowledge the late photographer John Margolies, who bequeathed his personal archive to the Library of Congress with the amazing stipulation that no restrictions were to be imposed on its use by other authors and researchers.

In 1973, your ten-year-old author poses with the sign outside the now long-gone Tales of the Okefenokee dark ride at Six Flags Over Georgia. The interior of the building was gutted in 1980 and converted into, first, the Monster Plantation and then today's Monster Mansion.

INTRODUCTION

Welcome, friends, to the latest volume in the ongoing Lost Attractions series. For those who are new in this neighborhood, perhaps it would be best to begin by explaining the title. Just what is a "lost attraction" of Georgia, anyway? Well, it is very simple. A "lost attraction" can be any type of tourism-related business—roadside attraction, motel, restaurant or other—that no longer exists. Casually flipping through the pages, one might conceivably run across an image and comment, "Hey, that place is still there!" That would bring us to a secondary definition: a business that has changed radically over the years and no longer resembles its depiction in vintage photos and postcards, even though, technically, it may still be operating. Everything clear now?

Moving through these pages, we are going to see that Georgia contained as wide a variety of attractions as any other state. A big difference, however, was in their distribution. Whereas states such as Florida or Tennessee tended to have cities or even larger geographical areas where attractions were concentrated, in Georgia, there was pretty much only one major tourist town: Atlanta. It will take several chapters for us to cover all the varied sights of that capital city, and even then, there are some that will spill over into subsequent chapters.

Outside of Atlanta's urban sprawl—which today sprawls even more than it did back then, but perhaps less urbanely—Georgia's other attractions tended to be spread widely apart along the numerous main highways that led south toward the border with Florida. Sometimes, there were obvious reasons why certain attractions sprouted where they did, but more often, there seemed to be no logical explanation. If there was a highway, and a good chance that carloads of families were going to be traveling on it en route to the white sand beaches, that seemed to be reason enough for someone to open a roadside zoo, a candy store or a mom-and-pop motel with a home-cooking restaurant attached.

I must sheepishly admit that my own family's experiences with Georgia tourism were largely confined to the aforementioned Atlanta metropolitan area. Living near Birmingham, Alabama, we rarely had a reason to explore the large swath of Georgia that lay between Atlanta and Florida; our travels to the Sunshine State normally took a different route. But, in June 1967, we did make a visit to the Okefenokee Swamp on our way to St. Augustine. Finding the marsh severely affected by a recent drought, we repeated the trip the following summer. My dad was shooting Polaroid photos during the 1967 trip, and I remember him posing me atop the large concrete amphibian that sat in front of Waycross's longstanding Green Frog Restaurant. That was some hot concrete in the June sun, and the fact that no resulting photo is in my archives undoubtedly means I did not stay still long enough for a photo—or the notoriously undependable Polaroid film malfunctioned in the heat.

But that was only one such attraction that no longer exists, and we are now about to see many, many others. From theme parks to zoos to colorful motels and pecan shops selling souvenirs, they all await just around the next bend in the road. Fasten your seat belts, and let's head out!

CHAPTER ONE

Capital Times in the Capital

It seems most logical to begin our tour of Georgia's defunct attractions in the state capital of Atlanta. As we shall see in the pages that follow, the vast majority of attractions in Georgia were concentrated in the Atlanta metro region—so many, in fact, that they will leak into other chapters that follow this one.

We might say that the first out-of-state visitors to Atlanta were the Union troops who fought their way into that strategic location during the Civil War. Of course, at that time, there were no amusement parks or miniature-golf courses waiting to help the soldiers pass the time; perhaps that is why they were so perturbed that they burned their way through the rest of the state to the coast at Savannah. (Ironically, millions of future tourists would follow roughly that same route on their way to the wonders of Florida.)

Even though we are about to get a heaping helping of Atlanta attractions, it must be acknowledged that there were others that should have been included, but the necessary material simply was not there. One of those was the Funland amusement park, made infamous in one of Martin Luther King's speeches. He correctly pointed out that his daughters could not enter its gates. That blemish aside, Funland operated for many years, and its ruins became something of a local landmark. But in preparing this book, we were unable to secure a single photo of reproducible quality. The same thing goes for the Tornado roller coaster that once loomed over the Lakewood Fairgrounds; usable photos of it escaped our clutches.

But, instead of concentrating on what is not here, let's dive into the smorgasbord that we were able to round up. Next stop, Atlanta!

PERENNIAL AND TROPICAL GARDENS — T H O M P S O N ' S   F L O R A L A N D — ATLANTA, GA.

OPPOSITE: In the early 1900s, Atlanta was home to a quite remarkable number of amusement parks. One of those was Ponce de León Park, which went through several different formats before closing in 1924. For a park that lasted fewer than twenty-five years, and more than a century ago, there are a surprising number of postcards still extant.

ABOVE: And speaking of plentiful postcards, this one from Thompson's Floraland turns up over and over again on the collectors' market. Just what the attraction was, or even where it was located, is unclear, except for a general description of it as a "perennial and tropical garden."

The most spectacular failure in Georgia amusement park history was the doomed World of Sid and Marty Krofft in downtown Atlanta, based on the television creations of the Krofft brothers. Opening with great fanfare in May 1976, it crashed with a resounding thud only six months later. *David Kelleher collection.*

OPPOSITE: The World of Sid and Marty Krofft was built inside Atlanta's newly opened Omni complex. Visitors rode a multistory escalator to the top floor and then worked their way down through the attractions on the lower levels. At the time of this photo, the usual ice-skating rink on the ground floor had been temporarily converted into a basketball court for the taping of a TV special.

ABOVE & OPPOSITE, TOP: One reviewer noted that if people were expecting the Krofft park to be "Six Flags Under Glass," they were much mistaken. With only a handful of rides, the park placed most of its emphasis on live performance, with puppeteers and mimes mingling with the crowds to give more of a carnival atmosphere.

OPPOSITE, BOTTOM: One of the Krofft park's few true amusement rides was this one, which simulated a trip through a larger-than-life pinball machine. A dark ride in the Omni's basement traveled through scenes from the Kroffts' hit TV series *H.R. Pufnstuf.*

Wow! You gotta see all the toys 'n pretty clothes! Mommy got me some books 'n candy. And Daddy played games and let me win. This place is fun!

When you see Omni International through the eyes of a child, you'll discover our shops filled with wondrous treasures. Many one-of-a-kind items, many good values, too. Come enjoy the fashions, books, sculpture, games and more – plus all the restaurants and fun – all under one fantastic roof Omni International.

Wow! OMNI INTERNATIONAL Marietta at Techwood and International Blvd.

OPPOSITE: Perceived high crime and a lack of traditional amusements doomed the World of Sid and Marty Krofft to an early demise in November 1976. By the time of this photo in December 1982, the ice-skating rink was still in use, but other traces of the defunct park had been removed.

LEFT: For its part, the Omni did its best to become a glorified shopping mall, with specialty shops and restaurants filling the space. Those, too, were gradually phased out as the property was taken over by the CNN Studios throughout the 1980s and 1990s.

BELOW: One huge part of the Krofft park lives on. When tourists take the tour at CNN Center today, they begin by riding the same escalator to the top floor, and a tour guide briefly explains its history for the thousands who have never heard of the World of Sid and Marty Krofft. *Dave Kelleher collection.*

OPPOSITE, TOP: The spectacular neon signage of the Blue Bird Truck Stop long predated any interstate highways—some sources say it went back to 1959. However, it truly became a downtown Atlanta landmark after the major thoroughfares I-20, I-75 and I-85 formed a junction near its location. *John Margolies collection.*

OPPOSITE, BOTTOM: From this angle, in the distance we can see the 1965 Atlanta–Fulton County Stadium, which was demolished in 1997 to make room for the new Turner Field's parking lot. In the foreground, note the once-familiar pitched orange roof of a Howard Johnson's Motor Lodge and Restaurant; we will be seeing more of that famous chain a little later.

ABOVE, LEFT: Another familiar motel chain, TraveLodge, hung out its sign in downtown Atlanta. The logo, the sleepwalking Sleepy Bear, had by that time been abstracted into a solid orange shape, but he was still identifiable as the comforting emblem of a place to catch some Zs.

ABOVE, RIGHT: Could anything better represent the opulence of the 1980s than this brochure for the downtown Atlanta Marriott Hotel? From the pool to the food to the couple working out together in the fitness center, these could be scenes from *Dynasty* or *Falcon Crest*.

OPPOSITE: Opening in 1969, Underground Atlanta was an entertainment and dining district utilizing the historic buildings that had been forgotten after the city's system of viaducts had been built overhead to handle traffic flow. As these maps showing the layout from two different angles indicate, there was a wide variety of bars, gift and craft shops, restaurants and entertainment venues. Facing problems similar to those that scuttled the World of Sid and Marty Krofft—primarily, crime in the area—Underground Atlanta had been buried and forgotten again by 1980. There have been sporadic attempts to revive it as a shopping district in recent years. *Tim Campbell collection.*

ABOVE: One of the many themed restaurants in Underground Atlanta was the Spanish Village, which, despite its name, specialized in Mexican cuisine rather than anything from Europe.

No tourist trap would be complete without a wax museum, and Underground Atlanta trapped its share of tourists with the three-story Josephine Tussaud Underground Wax Museum. It should probably come as no surprise that the brochure prominently featured those two Civil War combatants Lee and Grant, but the rest of the displays were much the same as could be found in the Tussaud chain's other museums in tourist hotspots across the country.

From 1948 until 1990, a downtown Atlanta tradition was the lighting of the giant Christmas tree atop the glass-enclosed walkways at Rich's department store. This highly stylized photo decorated the cover of a record album containing musical selections from the lighting ceremony. Although there is still a Great Tree each year, the old Rich's flagship store is long gone—as is the Rich's name.

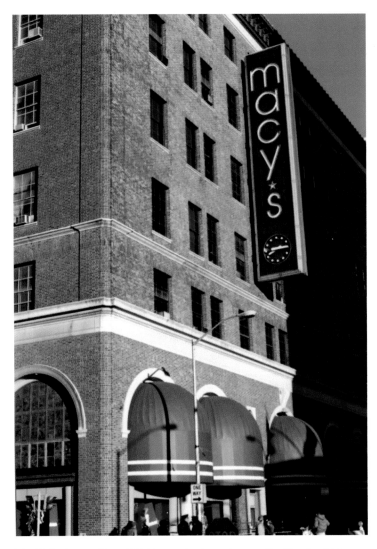

The chain that swallowed Rich's was the legendary retailer Macy's, which had long had its own presence in downtown Atlanta. It, too, is now gone, although, to its credit, Macy's has maintained the annual tree-lighting ceremony at Lenox Square.

OPPOSITE: Of course, the Macy's name is far more associated with its annual Thanksgiving Day Parade than with tree lightings, and for a few years in the mid-1980s, there was a Macy's Christmas Parade in downtown Atlanta. Some of the giant cartoon character balloons made the trip down from New York City to wend their way through Atlanta's canyons.

OPPOSITE TOP, LEFT: Meanwhile, during a different holiday season, the Atlanta Passion Play was presented each Easter from 1977 through 2011. The elaborate production was staged by Atlanta's First Baptist Church. *Mark Pedro collection.*

OPPOSITE TOP, RIGHT: The chain of Lion Country Safari parks had already set up outposts in Florida and California before someone made the questionable decision to bring the concept to central Georgia. This brochure announced the impending grand opening in the summer of 1972, using photos from the other locations.

OPPOSITE, BOTTOM: The entrance to Lion Country Safari, resembling two frighteningly huge elephant tusks, could be found on Walt Stephens Road in the Atlanta suburb of Stockbridge.

LEFT: The main feature at all Lion Country Safari parks was the experience of driving through the wildlife habitat for a close-up view of the free-ranging animals. In those pre-digital days, each carload would be furnished with a cassette tape player and a prerecorded spiel that described the sights to be seen, with appropriate instructions for when to start and stop the tape in order to keep the journey in sync.

In an attempt to increase its audience, in 1977, a number of amusement rides were added to Lion Country Safari, and the park's name was changed to the enigmatic Kingdoms Three. The safari drive remained but was no longer the mane (ha, ha) selling point. The park closed in 1984. Today, the original location in West Palm Beach, Florida, is the last surviving remnant of the chain.

OPPOSITE: Where the lions and other furred and feathered creatures once roamed, there is now a residential neighborhood known as Monarch Village (not named after the king of beasts, most likely). The only remnants of Lion Country Safari are some of the ponds that once made up parts of the habitat.

CHAPTER TWO

Old Times There Were Not Forgotten

Okay, it is now time to confront the dinosaur in the room. There is positively no way of avoiding the fact that an enormous number of Georgia attractions—not only in Atlanta but in the rest of the state as well—commemorated the Civil War era and Georgia's participation in that conflict. And one could hardly say that they presented a balanced view on the subject. No, sir, one and all presumed that 99.9 percent of their visitors would be thoroughly sympathetic to the "Lost Cause" of the Confederacy.

It is not our purpose here to psychoanalyze these one-sided antebellum-heavy attractions but simply to present them in the same context as all the others in this book: as relics of their time. The Civil War–themed sights in Georgia encompassed roadside attractions as well as restaurants and motels. If anyone is offended by the images that we have chosen to illustrate Atlanta's once-popular Mammy's Shanty restaurant, we can wholeheartedly assure you that there were infinitely more offensive ones we could have used.

As stated in the previous chapter, it was no doubt the Union soldiers who made up the first out-of-state visitors to Georgia in any large numbers. Why, then, were so many future attractions meant to remind everyone of the losing side, especially when so many tourists were coming down from the northern states? Perhaps W.S. Stuckey, of those ubiquitous pecan shoppes, summed it up best in a famous quote: "Thank God the North won that war. It would have been awful if there hadn't been any Yankees to sell to."

BE SURE AND
See
KENNESAW
BATTLE-RAMA

World's Finest
CIVIL WAR
DIORAMA and MUSEUM

LOCATED ON U.S. 41
at Kennesaw Mountain
18 MILES NORTH OF ATLANTA

LEFT: Among the most common attractions were the miniaturized battlefield dioramas upon which tiny troops would reenact famous conflicts. The Kennesaw Battle-Rama was one of these, naturally depicting the Battle of Kennesaw Mountain. It shared common ownership with the similarly named Confederama in Chattanooga and the Cherokee-Rama in Gatlinburg.

BELOW: The other Civil War memorials were dwarfed by the Atlanta Cyclorama, an enormous painting depicting that crucial conflict. Painted for a traveling exhibition, it moved to Atlanta in 1891 and thirty years later took up residence in this imposing building in Atlanta's Grant Park. Note the bas-relief friezes on either side of the entrance; later photos show that these were eventually removed and replaced by plain brickwork.

OPPOSITE: The Cyclorama is not technically a lost attraction, just a relocated one. Between 2015 and 2019, the entire setup was moved from Grant Park to the Atlanta History Center, where it remains on display. The 1921 Cyclorama building was renovated into office and event space for Zoo Atlanta.

Cyclorama Building, Atlanta, Ga.

FORT WALKER; original trenches and complete Confederate battery. The adjacent observation tower provides a magnificent view of Atlanta's everchanging skyline.

SPECTACULAR, SUPERB

CYCLORAMA

ATLANTA, GEORGIA
SEE AND HEAR
THE BATTLE OF ATLANTA
which took place east of
Atlanta, July 22, 1864.

LOCATION: Grant Park, in southeast Atlanta (see map).

HOURS: In winter—9:00 a.m. to 5:30 p.m. week-days, 9:00 a.m. to 6:00 p.m. Sundays; in summer—9:00 a.m. to 6:00 p.m. daily.

LECTURES: Every hour, on the half-hour, beginning at 9:30 a. m.

ADMISSION: $1.00 adults, 50c children, Includes tax.

GROUP RATES AVAILABLE

Another part of the Cyclorama in its Grant Park days was the actual *Texas* locomotive that played such a major role in the legendary "Great Locomotive Chase" against the captured *General* locomotive. The *Texas* was displayed in the basement of the Cyclorama building but later accompanied the painting on its move to the Atlanta History Center.

OPPOSITE, TOP: One of Georgia's most enduring contributors to American literature was Joel Chandler Harris, author of the stories about ex-slave Uncle Remus and his folk tales about Brer Rabbit. U.S. 441 was for many years designated as the Uncle Remus Route, due to the fact that it passed through Harris's birthplace of Eatonton. *Bob Cara collection.*

OPPOSITE, BOTTOM: Eatonton featured an Uncle Remus Restaurant—at which, in the days of segregation, non-Whites were not allowed to eat. It was even more ironic that the restaurant had a figure of Uncle Remus sitting in its front window. For this promotional photo, that figure was temporarily moved to Eatonton's main drag, which today is a lot less grassy than it appears here.

UNCLE REMUS ROUTE 441

Georgia's Most Direct Route

NORTH AND SOUTH

As a Memorial to Joel Chandler Harris, creator of the famed Uncle Remus stories, this picturesque route has been designated. Traversing a section of Georgia already popular with tourists and Georgians alike, this route not only offers a "short way north or south" but provides a scenic panorama that is refreshing and historical.

Such spots as Eatonton, the birthplace of Joel Chandler Harris; the Suwanee River; the Okefenokee Swamp; the University of Georgia; the Georgia State College for Women; South Georgia College and the Bright-leaf tobacco belt. These and many other beckon the tourist to pause on their journey and "come in and set a spell".

Traveling down through the Empire State, the lowly pine tree comes into its own and the working and chipping, the dipping of turpentine can be seen from the highway. Close to McRae, where is located two of the largest turpentine stills in the world, is Little Ocmulgee State Park.

Good hunting and fishing can be found along the Uncle Remus Route and the tourist has only to pack his gun, rod and reel and, of course, have a Georgia License to fish or hunt.

From McRae to Fargo the pine tree furnishes a living for many of the people in this section. Here the largest percentage of the world's Naval Stores are produced.

In Douglas is located the largest Junior College in the University System, having what is considered the most beautiful campus in Georgia. Douglas was the pioneer town in the bright-leaf tobacco Belt and the first barn for flue-curing tobacco in Georgia was built in Coffee County. Here also is a naval stores agricultural and livestock center and peanut market.

FOR ADDITIONAL INFORMATION ASK ANY CHAMBER OF COMMERCE ON THIS ROUTE OR WRITE HEADQUARTERS UNCLE REMUS ROUTE.

U. S. 441 Highway Association
Chamber of Commerce
Douglas, Ga.

RICH'S Children's Menu

OPPOSITE & ABOVE: Brer Rabbit could certainly be found not only in his briar patch but also in many other locations around middle Georgia. In his Disney rendition, he appeared on an antiques shop's signage in Eatonton, while at the Brer Rabbit Motel in nearby Dublin, he more closely resembled Bugs Bunny.

LEFT: An older-looking, bewhiskered Brer Rabbit served as the mascot for Atlanta's downtown Rich's children's menu. It boasted such dishes as the Brer Fox Lunch (sliced turkey), the Brer Wolf Lunch (chopped beefsteak) and Brer Rabbit's Baby Brother Lunch (choice of pureed foods or Gerber brand baby food).

It would have been almost impossible to completely ignore the Confederate theme in any part of Georgia, but especially in Atlanta. Johnny Reb's Restaurant looks like it might have denied service to anyone with a Yankee license plate. *John Margolies collection.*

The Stonewall Court on U.S. 41 at Smyrna looked something like the great-grandpa of the much later Cracker Barrel chain, with its display of early Georgia artifacts. Unfortunately, it burned in 1946, taking all of its historical relics with it.

From today's viewpoint, it is hard to know just what to say about Atlanta's famous Mammy's Shanty Restaurant, except that it dished up its dishes for some forty-three years before closing in January 1972. That colorful neon sign certainly made quite a contrast to the decidedly non-shanty-like appearance of the main building. Even Uncle Remus never had it that good.

12— "Lincoln Oak" near Radium Springs, Albany, Ga.

OA4305-N

OPPOSITE, TOP: One of Mammy's Shanty's most popular features—apart from the food— was its painting titled *The Surrender.* Yes, with all the components helpfully labeled, it depicted that improbable moment in history (?) when General Grant surrendered to General Lee. The image was so beloved that it was reproduced on a number of souvenirs sold in the Mammy's Shanty gift shop, including postcards and drinking glasses.

OPPOSITE, BOTTOM: For those traveling south from Savannah toward Florida on U.S. 17, there was the Plantation Inn and Motor Court, where each of the cabins sought to replicate an antebellum Southern mansion. *Marla Akin collection.*

ABOVE: By no means could it have been considered "equal time," but for those who were not on the side of the Confederacy, Albany offered the Lincoln Oak, uncannily shaped like the sixteenth president's profile. Presumably, natural growth ensured that this attraction would be lost sooner rather than later.

CHAPTER THREE

The Lost Worlds of Six Flags

Had it been our goal, we could have filled up an entire book with 180 images of parts of Six Flags Over Georgia that no longer exist. In fact, one almost has to use a microscope to locate any present-day elements of the park that were a part of its first decade, and even the ones that do still exist have been altered beyond all recognition.

When Six Flags opened in June 1967, it became the first true theme park in the Southeast. Its parent park, Six Flags Over Texas, unfurled its banners between Dallas and Fort Worth in 1961. Its theming was based on the six different countries whose flags had flown over that vast territory: Spain, France, Mexico, the Confederate States, the United States and the Texas flag itself.

When plans were made for a Georgia parallel, fortunately from a planning perspective, some of the flags still applied. In Georgia, Britain replaced Mexico, and of course there was the small matter that the Georgia state flag never represented an independent nation, as did the Texas state flag. But the rest were retained, and Six Flags Over Georgia in its original form became a living history lesson.

As the years went by and the public's tastes in entertainment changed, the historical themes receded further into the background. Add to that the problematic nature of having a section devoted to celebrating Georgia's antebellum Confederate period, and it is easy to see why the six original flags have been quietly retired. Today, the six flags that fly over the main gate are all the American flag, eliminating any embarrassing questions or comments. But we are about to visit the park in its original form, when each period of Georgia's history was represented by its own set of rides, shows, restaurants and shops. Let's jump on the parking lot tram and head for the ticket booths.

OPPOSITE: The Six Flags brand is so well known today that few people remember its original meaning. In Atlanta's case, the park was themed around the six flags that had flown over the territory during its history: those of Spain, France, Britain, the Confederacy, the United States of America and Georgia.

ABOVE: Sharp-eyed viewers might have noticed that in the six titular flags at the entrance, the Confederate states were not represented by the traditional battle flag but by the more official "Stars and Bars" design. Take another look: at this time, the battle flag still made up most of the Georgia state flag, so using it to represent the Confederacy would have resulted in two practically identical flags on those poles.

As this classic 1971 map shows, Six Flags Over Georgia was a vastly different place when its original theming was still in place. It resembled a Disney park far more than the thrill-ride-packed piece of property of today. Each of the flags had its own section of the park, with at least a nominal attempt to inform guests of some historical facts regarding each. At the top of the map, the Lickskillet section represented an early Georgia coal-mining town—the first section added that did not directly relate to the six other countries.

Six Flags certainly wasted no effort to promote its many attractions in those early years. Here, marketing whiz Bette Justice holds things down in the park's booth during a tourism industry trade show in Charlotte, North Carolina. *Bette Justice collection.*

OPPOSITE, TOP: This fountain and its classical statuary graced Six Flags' entrance plaza. Many rounds of subsequent remodeling eliminated the fountain, and at last report, the toga-clad ladies were being employed—minus their heads—as part of the park's annual Halloween decorations.

OPPOSITE, BOTTOM: Not everything at Six Flags was strictly based on Georgia history. These columns at the entrance, for example, were modeled after the ruins of a former plantation house known as Windsor, located not in the Peach State but in southern Mississippi.

In the early 1970s, this motley crew of costumed characters could be found roaming the park. In this classic publicity photo, the bizarre personalities from Sid and Marty Kroffts' Saturday morning *H.R. Pufnstuf* and *Lidsville* series are joined by commercial spokesman W.C. Fritos. *Andy Duckett collection.*

OPPOSITE, TOP: During Six Flags' first few years, the most famous attraction was the Log Jamboree flume ride. One of the lifts featured a close encounter with this melodramatic villain, complete with cape, top hat and sneer, sawing a log that threatened to fall onto the boats below.

OPPOSITE, BOTTOM: For the park's 1968 season, a second log flume ride was added to help handle the crowds. It, too, featured an animated giant, this time a brutish version of Paul Bunyan chopping away with his axe. *Tim Campbell collection.*

The 1968 flume also had a final drop through this simulated hollow log. Although the original 1967 flume was demolished long ago, the 1968 flume still operates—although without the colorful presence of Paul Bunyan and the log tunnel. *Shaunnon Drake collection.*

The Crystal Pistol music hall presented re-creations of the type of entertainment one might have seen in antebellum Georgia, along with more modern stage presentations. Today, it still features some live performances, but not of the historical nature seen here.

The centerpiece of Six Flags' Confederate section was the Tales of the Okefenokee dark ride, bringing to animated life the characters from the old plantation legends. Its debt to Joel Chandler Harris was obvious, even though Harris had placed his stories in middle Georgia's Putnam County, not Ware County's swamplands.

The version of Tales of the Okefenokee that first-year park visitors saw in 1967 was quite different from what it later became. The original animated figures were tiny, about the size of department store window decorations, and their limited movements were clumsy, to say the least. *Manuel Fernandez collection.*

For the 1968 season, Six Flags employed Sid and Marty Krofft to completely revamp the Okefenokee ride with larger-than-life animated figures more closely resembling something out of Disneyland. This version operated until the end of the 1980 season, at which point everything in the building—except the trough in which the boats ran—was bulldozed for a new dark ride, the Monster Plantation. *Manuel Fernandez collection.*

The brothers Krofft had their talented hands all over Six Flags for many years. Their showcase was a puppet theater with an animated façade representing architecture from around the world. It was their success at Six Flags that prompted the Kroffts to open their own trouble-ridden park in downtown Atlanta, as seen in chapter one. *Tim Campbell collection.*

Inside the Krofft Puppet Theatre, elaborate marionette productions were staged. They usually highlighted celebrity caricatures—sometimes with the stars providing their own prerecorded voices—but at other times, the Kroffts' TV output, including H.R. Pufnstuf himself, could be seen.

OPPOSITE, TOP: After Sid and Marty Krofft departed for the Omni, the gap in Six Flags' puppetry was filled by insult comic Buford Buzzard. No one was safe from his barbed comments, which were usually hilarious except to the easily offended. *Tim Campbell collection.*

OPPOSITE, BOTTOM & ABOVE: The Six Flags porpoise show was one attraction that did not seem to fit into any of the prescribed sections. It sat on the border of the Spain section and the French section, belonging to neither. As these photos indicate, through the years, the appearances of the female porpoise trainers evolved, but the two lovable aquatic mammals, Skipper and Dolly, remained basically the same from beginning to end.

Six Flags' parallel to Disney's Jungle Cruise was Jean Ribaut's Adventure, an outdoor boat ride through two hundred years of Georgia history. Each trip culminated in the boats facing the blazing cannons of the British stronghold at Fort Argyle. In 1981, Ribaut became a part of history and the canal was dredged and widened to become the whitewater rafting ride Thunder River. *Both, Manuel Fernandez collection.*

OPPOSITE, TOP: Another Six Flags feature with origins outside Georgia was the Spanish section's Castillo de Soto. Its physical appearance was based on the Castillo de San Marcos at St. Augustine, Florida—although, for some reason, that historic site lacked hot-pink turrets.

OPPOSITE, BOTTOM: The main attraction inside the Spanish fort was the Horror Cave, accessed by entering over the tongue and into the gaping maw of an evil-looking head.

ABOVE: The unsettling animated dioramas in the Horror Cave were more creations by Sid and Marty Krofft, far removed from the whimsical fun of the Okefenokee or the puppet theater. In this scene, a maniacal Mr. Hyde type and his Tor Johnson look-alike helper gleefully display the severed head of a woman in her red velvet plush bedroom. Yikes! *Manuel Fernandez collection.*

TOP: A huge piece of real estate in the USA section was occupied by the Happy Motoring Freeway, sponsored by the Humble Oil Company throughout its various brand-name changes from Esso to Enco to Exxon. At far right, note the rendition of the "Tiger in Your Tank" emblem perched on the corner of the canopy. *Nelson Boyd collection.*

BOTTOM: This angle not only shows how much space the Happy Motoring Freeway occupied but also gives a glimpse of two other lost attractions: the giant Sky Hook ride and the Chevy Show, a theater with a 180-degree screen that took up the audience's entire field of vision.

OPPOSITE: After the 1976 season, the freeway was plowed under. In its place rose the Great Gasp, a parachute drop ride whose origins can be traced back to the 1939 New York World's Fair. It was the tallest structure in the park until even higher roller coasters replaced it.

OPPOSITE, TOP: Also in the USA section was Petsville, a zoo area in which cute kids and even cuter young animals could interact with each other.

OPPOSITE, BOTTOM: At one time, scattered throughout the park were movie theater–style posters advertising the various attractions to be seen. Here, photographed at dusk, the Tales of the Okefenokee poster promotes the never-ending conflict between Mr. Rabbit, Mr. Fox and Mr. Bear. *Tim Campbell collection.*

ABOVE: When Six Flags added the Cotton States Exposition section in 1973, it was named for a famous Atlanta exhibition held in 1895. The main feature of that section was the Great American Scream Machine coaster, and thus it might be seen as the beginning of the end for Six Flags' original historical theme and its transition to thrill rides almost exclusively.

CHAPTER FOUR

More Than a Carving

In addition to the many Civil War–themed attractions we visited back in chapter two, the biggest and most visible was the Confederate monument chiseled out of solid granite on the side of Stone Mountain, a few miles east of Atlanta. Work on that carving occupied a long stretch from 1923 to 1970, although there were many years between those two when nothing was being done.

The original Stone Mountain carver was Gutzon Borglum, but he got only as far as General Robert E. Lee's head before running into conflicts with the powers in charge. Borglum washed the Stone Mountain granite dust off his hands and made tracks for the Black Hills of South Dakota, where he literally carved out his own place in history with the four presidential faces on Mount Rushmore.

In 1925, New York artist Augustus Lukeman took over the Stone Mountain project, and his first order of action was to blast away Borglum's completed Lee head and start all over. He, too, barely got about half of Lee finished before the lease on the mountain ran out, and work was halted in 1928.

It was probably the revival of Confederate pride arising from the burgeoning civil rights movement that prompted the state to purchase Stone Mountain in 1958 and begin building park facilities there. Work on the carving did not resume until 1962, and it was finally unveiled and considered complete in 1970. ("Considered" complete, because the finished carving still ended at the horses' stomachs, leaving their lower extremities to the imagination.)

Just as at Six Flags, Stone Mountain Park has hosted numerous features that no longer exist and others whose presentation and marketing have changed drastically. We will now step back in time and see just what the state had to offer tourists besides a look at a carving that was seemingly always in progress.

Stone Mountain 16 Miles East of Atlanta, the largest solid Rock in te World, Atlanta, Ga.

Prior to 1923, this is how Stone Mountain, a huge granite outcropping, would have appeared to anyone who happened to be in its neighborhood. After much planning, that was the year work finally got underway on a carving to commemorate those three heroes of the Confederacy: Robert E. Lee, Jefferson Davis and Stonewall Jackson.

OPPOSITE: Even before the carving began to take shape, postcards were being issued to show planned improvements at Stone Mountain that never existed in real life. One was this Confederate Memorial Hall and reflecting pool, shown underneath a proposed version of the carving that was about three times the size of the final project.

SHOWING STATUE OF "MEMORY." TO BE DEDICATED TO WOMEN OF CONFEDERACY.

DETAIL OF GRAND STAIRWAY LEADING UP TO MEMORIAL HALL, SHOWING BRONZE INCENSE URN.

This unusual double-view postcard further illustrated the impractical Memorial Hall, which was to have been drilled 60 feet deep into the mountain's base. At 320 feet above the sidewalk, it was to require a long flight of steps to reach the columned entrance.

OPPOSITE, TOP: The carving on the side of the mountain was also pictured in many different configurations, all of which were fictitious. This one showed the three main figures backed by flag bearers and further mounted troops.

OPPOSITE, BOTTOM: As practical considerations became necessary, the intended carving was whittled down. This 1936 version left only one mounted horseman behind Lee, Davis and Jackson. Their pose, with their hats over their hearts, was a remnant of the earlier design, in which they were saluting the Confederate flag they had just passed. Now the flag was gone but the salute remained.

Stone Mountain, where the Confederate Memorial is being Chiseled in Solid Granite, Atlanta, Ga.

121— DAVIS, LEE, JACKSON AND COLOR BEARER IN MASTER MODEL FOR CENTRAL GROUP

Work on the carving stopped in 1928 and did not resume until 1962, by which time the state had purchased the mountain and its surrounding property and turned it into Stone Mountain State Park. The finished carving was unveiled in 1970, although it still showed the figures only from the horses' stomachs up. In 1997, Georgia ceded control of Stone Mountain Park to Herschend Entertainment, of Silver Dollar City and Dollywood fame.

OPPOSITE: When Stone Mountain State Park opened in 1958, since work on the carving had been halted for three decades, other attractions had to fill the void. The first, and most heavily promoted, was the Stone Mountain Scenic Railroad. One might have expected it to carry a Civil War theme, but in fact it did not. Instead, it dragged out the hackneyed settlers–versus–Native Americans plot, with actors staging the action at appropriate spots along the route.

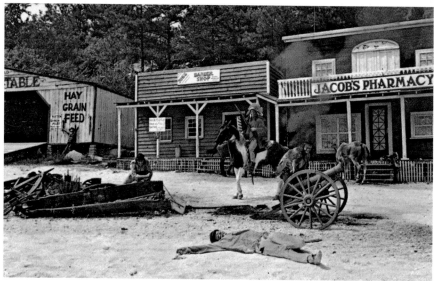

This could very well be the corniest postcard ever produced by a major Georgia attraction. As you can probably surmise, the phony chief has supposedly just "scalped" an unfortunate victim with an even more phony and unconvincing bald skullcap under his "hair." Most of the passengers seem to be finding it inexplicably humorous.

OPPOSITE, TOP: Most of the war-party action took place around a replica of the northwestern Georgia town of Ringgold, which likely never had trouble from local Native Americans dressed in the garb of the Plains Indians. Somehow, the marauders managed to burn the same red schoolhouse several times each day.

OPPOSITE, BOTTOM: Another added attraction was a sky lift to Stone Mountain's summit. It departed ground level from this futuristic, Jetsons-style launchpad. A museum and observation tower awaited atop the granite monolith.

OPPOSITE, TOP: Another feature on Stone Mountain's peak was this memorial, somewhat reminiscent of the original plans for the base of the mountain. Above a reflecting pool flew the flags of the former Confederate states.

OPPOSITE, BOTTOM: There were plans to renovate the mountaintop to welcome the overflow tourists from the 1996 Atlanta Olympic Games. However, once the observation tower and reflecting pool were demolished, nothing was built to take their place. This was how the former pool appeared in 2008.

ABOVE: During the 1960s, the park's reconstructed southern plantation was known as Stone Acres. The plantation is still very much a part of the park, but it now takes a more historically accurate approach, rather than the romanticized *Gone with the Wind*—type theme seen in this publicity shot.

Earlier, we had a brief glimpse at the attractions that played out history in tabletop dioramas. To that list we can add Stone Mountain's "Battlarena," which portrayed Georgia's role in the Civil War—both as a winner and as a loser.

OPPOSITE: The creation of Stone Mountain Lake as part of the state park development not only covered much of the original route of U.S. 78, which formerly passed directly by the granite peak, but also provided another venue for entertainment, notably the paddle-wheel showboat *Robert E. Lee*.

While "waiting on the *Robert E. Lee*," to quote a famous song title, tourists could explore Mark Twainland, whose name seemed to promise more than it delivered. It is barely remembered today, and this map makes it appear to be a smaller version of Disneyland's more famous Tom Sawyer Island.

OPPOSITE: The Game Ranch was a concession in the state park that offered up-close and personal encounters with a variety of wildlife. Although it was popular enough to rate its own separate line of souvenirs—the Scenic Railroad was another example of that trend—the Game Ranch always seemed to fly under the radar. It quietly closed down and slunk back into the forest in 2001.

A longer-lasting park concession was the Antique Auto Museum. Taking a cue from the famous Early American Museum at Silver Springs, Florida, the Stone Mountain attraction quickly moved beyond vintage vehicles and expanded into turn-of-the-century nostalgia in general.

Dioramas such as this one, with somewhat creepy mannequins, helped put the historical artifacts into perspective. All that was needed to make this one complete was a white dog to cock its head toward the gramophone's loudspeaker.

The Auto Museum's gift shop was somewhat unusual in that, along with the usual souvenirs, it also carried a selection of true antiques and collectibles, enabling those with enough money to take some of the items seen in the displays home with them.

And then there were the incongruous park attractions. On Stone Mountain Lake, kids could paddle around in the goggle-eyed Molly Whale Boats. Why a whale? Why was she named Molly? Those questions remained unanswered, but Stone Mountain Park, under the Herschend ownership, has managed to survive through some radically changing times.

CHAPTER FIVE

Georgia's Peachy Roadside

As we have seen, a big chunk of Georgia's attractions was found in the Atlanta metro area. But south of Atlanta, there was a vast expanse that hosted its own plethora of tourist-type goodies. The biggest difference was that Atlanta was a destination all its own, while the rest of the state was—to put it bluntly—a place tourists passed through on their way to the palm trees and sunny beaches of Florida.

Of course, most other southeastern states could have been considered in the same category, as none could even hope to come close to duplicating Florida's long-established tourist industry. The biggest difference for Georgia was that it bordered Florida, so that long haul from Atlanta to the state line was likely to be the final step for those who had driven a long way from Chicago or other northern climes.

That slog through middle and southern Georgia was even longer in the pre-interstate days, when all that traffic was funneled down U.S. 41, U.S. 27, U.S. 301 and the other legendary highways of their day. That meant that just about any town had the capability of developing some sort of attraction that had a good chance of survival just by being there to give those bleary-eyed travelers a reason to stop.

In this chapter, we are going to follow in those travelers' tire marks and drop in on a seemingly endless variety of museums, amusement parks, miniature-golf courses and souvenir shops—and other types that defy easy description. This is where we really start to see the ingenuity that existed among roadside entrepreneurs, so just grab a Stuckey's pecan roll and enjoy the ride!

GEORGIA
Year 'round vacation wonderland

LEFT: Sometimes, "lost" is a term that can apply to a general style of tourism promotion as much as to specific attractions. This 1960s brochure from the Georgia Tourism Department is very much a product of its time, although the model it chose looks tough enough to be an empowered woman of the twenty-first century.

OPPOSITE, TOP: Somehow, it is difficult to think of Marietta as a winter resort. However, when the original of this booklet was published in 1887, there were no highways—because there were no automobiles—so the railroad had its own interests in promoting the town northwest of Atlanta as a destination.

OPPOSITE, BOTTOM: Founded in 1856, Augusta's Fruitland Nurseries was not only an attraction but also a booming mail-order catalog business. After ceasing operations in 1918, the former Fruitland property was converted into the Augusta National Golf Club, site of the internationally famous Masters tournament.

Over the years, Okefenokee Swamp Park at Waycross has shifted between being a commercial attraction and one focusing more on nature. At the time of this postcard, the twig-like entrance sign was meant to convey the idea of what awaited inside the gate.

By 1968, this geometric spectacular of a sign marked the park's entrance on U.S. 1, looking more like the logo of a theme park. Incidentally, this photo was taken by your author when he was five years old, and that is his father pointing at the mammoth signage above.

RIGHT: The Okefenokee boat ride provided visitors with a number of sights, both natural and man-made. This macabre poem from skeletal "Billy Bones" was sure to provide a cheery way to brighten everyone's day.

BELOW: After facing Billy Bones's dire warning, Okefenokee boaters might have felt in need of some refreshment from this re-creation of the moonshine stills that thrived in the swamp's inaccessible depths. In our next chapter, we shall see how this impenetrable marsh influenced other businesses in the Waycross region.

In the days before most people ever thought about animal welfare, roadside zoos were a common sight. South of Richmond Hill on U.S. 17, Chico's Monkey Farm followed the grand tradition of billboards stretching for miles on either side. This lone example was captured by photographer John Margolies in the late 1970s, around the time the attraction took its bananas and went home. *John Margolies collection.*

OPPOSITE, TOP: Somewhat strangely, another wild animal park/zoo could be seen near Richmond Hill on U.S. 17. Its moniker of Dixie Jungle left no doubt that it was considered a true native son of Georgia. Apparently, it and Chico's Monkey Farm were separate, though quite similar, attractions in the same neighborhood—hardly an unheard-of situation in the tourist world.

OPPOSITE, BOTTOM: In a vastly different part of the state, the Georgia Game Park at Rising Fawn gradually evolved out of a roadside fireworks stand that also specialized in chenille bedspreads. By the 1960s, U.S. 11 was lined with billboards promoting its out-of-the-ordinary animals, including a five-legged dog and a six-legged cow.

OPPOSITE, TOP: After I-59 took all the tourists away from U.S. 11, the Georgia Game Park picked up its freaky beasts and moved over to the nearest interstate exit. Even after the property had become a truck stop, during the 1980s, the high fence with its fading Game Park signage could still be seen.

OPPOSITE, BOTTOM: Back on U.S. 11, this is how the original Georgia Game Park building appeared in November 2018. Its deformed denizens may be gone, but to judge from online comments, it seems that more people's memories focus on this location than on the later interstate incarnation.

ABOVE: Remember what we said about similar attractions tending to glom onto the same tourist areas? Also on U.S. 11 at Rising Fawn was this Georgia Deer Park, with its own live animal collection. And, since much of the passing traffic was on its way to the wonders of Lookout Mountain, note the two different sizes of Rock City birdhouses visible here.

LEFT: One of the most lost of all the lost Georgia attractions is Storyland, which spun its fairy tales at Marietta in the early 1960s. This brochure, with a Mother Goose who looks more like a witch, is identical to one used by another Storyland in Cape Cod, Massachusetts, clueing us in that they likely shared common ownership.

BELOW: Whatever one's opinion of Storyland's collection of storybook statuary, its entrance on U.S. 41 could not be missed. That stretch of highway has become so urbanized in the decades since that no visual indicators remain to memorialize where Ma Goose, Humpty Dumpty and their compatriots hung out. *Marietta Museum of History collection.*

Since the largest part of Georgia, the enormous section south of Atlanta, was primarily an area that tourists passed through on their way to or from Florida, it was up to numerous small attractions to give those tourists somewhere to stop. River Bend Park at Albany was a good example, with gas, food and lodging augmented by kiddie amusement rides for youngsters itching to get out of the back seat for a spell.

Callaway Gardens looks much the same today as it did fifty years ago, but some of the man-made elements have seen changes. One is the train ride, which still runs but no longer sports this miniature diesel locomotive look.

Laksa the Elephant was such an attraction at Albany's Tift Park Zoo that together they made the cover of the 1975 city phone directory. It was only a few years later that Laksa packed her trunk and, along with the rest of the outmoded zoo's exhibits, made tracks for a new, more habitable animal park in nearby Chehaw.

A sad reminder of tourism's bygone days is this rusting playground equipment at a once-bustling motel/restaurant complex at Unadilla. Even though it sat at the junction of U.S. 41 and busy I-75, apparently, it was intended to serve a demand that no longer existed, as the rest of the buildings on the property were also abandoned and overgrown when photographed in October 2017.

Museum of the Hills

PRESENTS
"THE STORY OF HELEN"

Our animated character, Barney O'Feller introduces you to an incomparable visit to the picturesque lifestyles of the hill country people in the South at the turn of the century.

Within the quaint castle building which houses the museum is a self-guided stroll down the country lanes and village streets and even into a farm home of these independent, rugged yet loving people. Take your time to sightsee, to inspect, to relax and be fascinated in air conditioned comfort.

Here you can absorb the charm of the old wood cookstove and accessories in the family kitchen, peek into grandma's chicken house for eggs, explore the interior of the stable, see a country marriage in progress. Special recordings throughout describe this entertaining, refreshing, and educational theme.

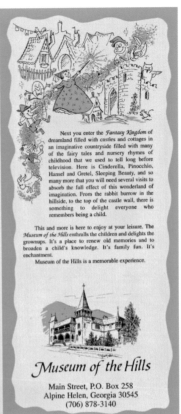

Next you enter the *Fantasy Kingdom* of dreamland filled with castles and cottages in an imaginative countryside filled with many of the fairy tales and nursery rhymes of childhood that we used to tell long before television. Here is Cinderella, Pinocchio, Hansel and Gretel, Sleeping Beauty, and so many more that you will need several visits to absorb the full effect of this wonderland of imagination. From the rabbit burrow in the hillside, to the top of the castle wall, there is something to delight everyone who remembers being a child.

This and more is here to enjoy at your leisure. The *Museum of the Hills* enthralls the children and delights the grownups. It's a place to renew old memories and to broaden a child's knowledge. It's family fun. It's enchantment.

Museum of the Hills is a memorable experience.

Museum of the Hills

Main Street, P.O. Box 258
Alpine Helen, Georgia 30545
(706) 878-3140

OPPOSITE, TOP: When the mountain town of Helen decided to reinvent itself with an Alpine theme, most of the businesses followed that lead. Some, such as the Museum of the Hills, got a little more out there. Its walk-through exhibit started out by relating the history of the area and then transitioned into the Fantasy Kingdom, which outdid the long-forgotten Storyland in its fairy-tale dioramas. *Mark Pedro collection.*

OPPOSITE, BOTTOM: For an attraction that was so colorful, research has turned up precious few photos of the Fantasy Kingdom. This one must be presumed to be fairly representative, with a solemn-looking Hansel and Gretel debating whether to knock on the door of the candy house or just eat their way through it. *Doug Kirby collection.*

RIGHT: Now, about Helen's World of Dreams Museum....You know something is up when an attraction's brochures fail to give a clue as to what lies inside and rely on a slogan along the lines of "You Won't Believe What You Will See." Apparently, not enough people believed they wanted to see it. *Mark Pedro collection.*

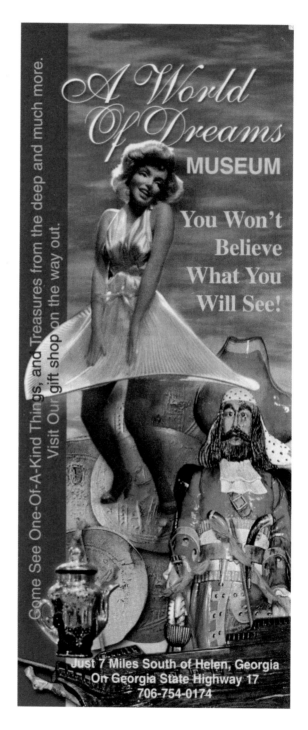

Come See One-Of-A-Kind Things, and Treasures from the deep and much more. Visit Our gift shop on the way out.

A World Of Dreams

MUSEUM

You Won't Believe What You Will See!

Just 7 Miles South of Helen, Georgia
On Georgia State Highway 17
706-754-0174

OPPOSITE, TOP: Now, if you were passing through Madison, on U.S. 441, and saw this building, with a stars-and-planets sign out front, what might be the last thing you would expect to find inside? If you answered "mosaics of famous incidents from the Bible," you would be correct. *Mark Pedro collection.*

OPPOSITE, BOTTOM: The colorful mosaics inside the misnamed Space View building were the work of artist Karl Steele. They had spent their previous life as part of the attraction known as the Rainforest on U.S. 301 near Wildwood, Florida. After that park closed around 1970, the artwork made an exodus for Georgia, but its subsequent wanderings in the wilderness seem to be undocumented. *Mark Pedro collection.*

ABOVE: This gift shop on U.S. 1, near Okefenokee Swamp Park, was almost a miniature theme park thanks to its variety of statuary. This postcard was mailed in November 1951, which gives particular significance to the row of pink flamingoes behind the birdbath. It is generally acknowledged that the traditional plastic flamingo decoration was not invented until 1957, leaving the existence of these some six years earlier a rosy-hued mystery.

Sometime in the late 1970s or early 1980s, photographer John Margolies captured this image of a steamboat-shaped welcome center at Darien. Unfortunately, that seems to be its only documentation. *John Margolies collection.*

OPPOSITE, TOP: Sometimes, things did not need to be an attraction to become a lost attraction. Sights like this retail strip in the appropriately named hamlet of Commerce were common in small towns across the state and the nation, but you will not encounter them today. The blue-and-orange front of a Rexall drugstore and its next-door neighbor, Harper's Five and Ten, are truly relics of a vanished era.

OPPOSITE, BOTTOM: Local banks have fared somewhat better than Rexall stores and five-and-dimes, although, usually, they have been merged into larger banking conglomerates. We were unable to learn the fate of the Citizens and Southern National Bank in Macon, which groomed itself as "the world's one and only Crystal Palace bank," issuing postcards to show off its Victorian theme.

Another town that played up the old-timey days was Hamilton, just a few miles from Callaway Gardens. Hamilton still promotes its history today, but the conglomeration of museums in this brochure seems to have disappeared into yesterday. Hopefully, their priceless collections have simply moved on to other attractions in other tourist locales.

OPPOSITE: In the northeastern Georgia mountains, the Old Sautee Store continues to capture the feeling of a bygone era. However, at one time, it was adjoined by the Yule Log Christmas Shop, described on its postcards as "a Norwegian log cabin with traditional grass roof." That must explain why it also had a goat on the roof.

The chain of Jolly Golf miniature-golf courses began in Gatlinburg in 1961 as a joint project of the Craddock and Sidwell families. Much later, Jim Sidwell chose Marietta as the site for another link in the chain, bringing his patented obstacles shaped like prehistoric beasts to those passing by on U.S. 41. *Both, Sidwell family collection.*

Mini-golf could sprout anywhere there were tourists, and it did not have to be as eye-popping as Jolly Golf. These two courses on Jekyll Island illustrate the simpler style of the game, although one of them scores extra points for employing a retired fiberglass Sinclair dinosaur as an obstacle.

OPPOSITE, TOP: Speaking of the beach, Georgia's relatively short coastline made the most of its location with traditional small seaside resorts. This view of the businesses (and at least one small amusement park) on Tybee Island makes one almost able to smell the salt air.

OPPOSITE, MIDDLE: Different types of smells are evoked by this alternate view from Tybee Island—namely, suntan lotion, cocoa butter and shampoo, possibly "Gee, Your Hair Smells Terrific."

OPPOSITE, BOTTOM: No, Rock City Gardens—atop Lookout Mountain, just over the Georgia state line from Chattanooga—is not a lost attraction and likely never will be. But over its long history it has had various elements that no longer exist, one of which is this Deer Park seen in 1967. More than thirty years later, the white fallow deer were moved to a more hospitable environment than this rocky pit.

ABOVE: For a brief period around 2013, a former souvenir stand was converted into a meet-and-greet area with Rock City's longtime mascot character, Rocky the Elf.

OPPOSITE, TOP: Deep inside Fairyland Caverns was Crystal Falls, in a room with walls and ceiling covered in genuine coral. Eventually, the weight of the coral weakened the supports to the point that Crystal Falls had to be blocked off and replaced with a display saluting Fairyland Caverns' original designer, Jessie Sanders.

OPPOSITE, BOTTOM: Traditionally, the last sight along Rock City's Enchanted Trail was the gristmill and its crew of colorful gnomes. In 1999, the wood structure burned to the ground, and today only its rotating waterwheel remains to mark its former location.

ABOVE: Now, let's stop for a while and visit those omnipresent roadside stands selling nuts, candy, souvenirs and other such necessities for a long trip. The pioneer of them all, at least in Georgia, was B. Lloyd's Pecan Service Stations. This advertising postcard was issued in 1941, just before World War II curtailed pleasure travel. As you can see, by that point, B. Lloyd's had outlets throughout southern Georgia and into adjoining states.

Let's face it: an entire book could be devoted to the history of Stuckey's—and, in fact, a couple of them have been. Beginning in 1937, Stuckey's spread its yellow-and-red billboards across Georgia and, eventually, the whole U.S.A. This fading example was somewhere along U.S. 17 in the late 1970s. *John Margolies collection.*

OPPOSITE, TOP: This was a typical example of 1950s Stuckey's building style, found at Richmond Hill, in the general vicinity of Dixie Jungle and Chico's Monkey Farm. The pink walls, murals advertising fresh orange juice and Texaco gas were standard elements of most stores in the chain.

OPPOSITE, BOTTOM: While the Stuckey's chain survives, many of its locations have not. This empty building sits on the site of the first Stuckey's store in Eastman; although it is a later 1960s design that replaced the original, it still bears a historical marker explaining its role in roadside history.

During John Margolies's meanderings through Georgia, he documented these two ruins of non-Stuckey's pecan shops. The yellow building copying Stuckey's color scheme was somewhere near Waverly; its more dilapidated relative was barely standing near Kingsland. *Both, John Margolies collection.*

For several years, Stuckey's closest rival was Horne's, begun by a former Stuckey's employee. Whereas Stuckey's eventually became known for its teal-colored roofs, Horne's used loud yellow roof tiles. In some former locations, including this one between Jesup and Nahanta, the yellow roof is the only thing left to indicate its former life. *Russell Wells collection.*

The exit for Cecil on I-75 was unusual in that it had a Stuckey's on the northbound side and a Horne's on the southbound side. Well into the twenty-first century, this rusted remnant of the Horne's signage could be seen next to the long-vacant lot.

OPPOSITE: Another small chain built on the Stuckey's business model was Candyland. It had fewer locations, but they stood out thanks to their peppermint-striped rooflines. Ironically, the Candyland at the Georgia/Florida border on I-75 eventually joined the Stuckey's family, but in 2017, it was again empty and awaiting its next identity.

ABOVE: Some former gift shops proved to be infinitely adaptable to other uses. This one on I-75 served as an antiques store for many years, but at last report its shelves and showcases were as empty as the gas tanks in the cars that once stopped under its canopy.

CHAPTER SIX

Sleepy Time Down South

If you're feeling a bit exhausted after visiting all of the varied attractions we just experienced, maybe that's a sign that it's time to check into a motel for the night. Just as with the attractions, roadside lodging could take a multitude of different forms, and the examples we have chosen to present here are only a tiny sampling. There could be hundreds more if only the space permitted.

Along with the motels, we will be seeing those other two businesses that were equally as necessary on any long road trip: gas stations and restaurants. It should probably come as no surprise to learn that the truly savvy businesspeople in the tourist trade often combined the three, so tourists could refill the gas tank, have a hearty meal and then bed down for the night all in the same roadside complex.

We normally think of vintage motels in terms of the independent mom-and-pop variety, and it is true that for a long time those were the most common. Even when chain motels such as Holiday Inn did appear on the scene, their early styles seem so quaint today that they fit right in with their nonchain counterparts. Who could forget peering into the darkness for the first glimmer of Holiday Inn's neon spectacular known officially as the Great Sign, flashing comfortingly in green, yellow, blue, pink and white and indicating that a soft, comfortable bed was only minutes away?

So, with these long-ago images of gas, food and lodging, we will close this look at Georgia's long- (or sometimes not-so-long-) vanished roadside attractions. Happy motoring to all, and to all a good night!

OPPOSITE, TOP: There is possibly no more evocative emblem of the early days of roadside lodging than this 1934 postcard from U.S. 41 in Valdosta. This particular copy was postmarked in December 1936, and the message to the recipient in Englewood, Tennessee, reads in part: "Drove 400 miles today—Stopped long before night—Staying at this camp tonight." You'll give yourself a treat if you pause reading here and simply wander around in this classic image.

OPPOSITE, BOTTOM: Travelers could not have made it from one motel to the next without the trusty "filling stations" along the way. The 1933 Shell road map of Georgia pairs nicely with this crumbling plastic example of the Shell emblem that was somehow hanging in there between Glenville and Ludowici, dating from long before its abstraction into a shape barely recognizable as a seashell. *Author's collection; Russell Wells collection.*

ABOVE: You probably need to look closely at this one to fully appreciate it. Note the unintended juxtaposition of the Sinclair service station and its prehistoric logo, its premium offer of an inflatable Dino beach toy and the sign pointing the way to (where else?) Flintstone, Georgia. Yabba dabba doo!

Regardless of what this brochure might have indicated, the DeSoto Hotel was not located on the beach but in downtown Savannah. (Note that, quite incidentally, the artwork is also promoting its saltier companion, the DeSoto Beach Club.)

OPPOSITE, TOP: Although Savannah still has a DeSoto Hotel, it is not the same building shown here. This one operated from 1890 until 1965, at which time it was demolished to make way for the current structure.

OPPOSITE, BOTTOM: Away from Savannah, on the genuine beach, the motels of Jekyll Island took on such variety in their signage that this collage was featured in a mid-1960s guide booklet. Note the Carriage Inn, representing an all-too-short-lived attempt by Stuckey's to cash in on its pecans in the lodging trade.

Dr. H. N. Alford . . . Owner

1266 Dixie Highway   Phone 478-6060

Jonesboro, Georgia

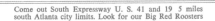

Come out South Expressway U. S. 41 and 19 5 miles south Atlanta city limits. Look for our Big Red Roosters

Today, U.S. 41/19, the Dixie Highway, at Jonesboro, is so urbanized that it seems unlikely for anyone to find anything resembling this cozy-sounding Farm House Restaurant and Motel. This letterhead encourages us to "look for our big red roosters." Unfortunately, this is all we have to see at the moment.

Saxon's was an Alabama-based chain of restaurants and candy stores in the Stuckey's or Horne's vein. This billboard on U.S. 41 was located thirty-two miles from either Perry or Cartersville; Saxon's had locations in both towns, so it is hard to say which.

This shell of a once-popular restaurant, and its towering neon sign, became a landmark on U.S. 301 at Dover long after it ceased to operate. This photo was made in May 2013, but since then, the property has been cleared for—surprise—a Dollar General store. The Paradise would have been an infinitely more unique occupant for the site.

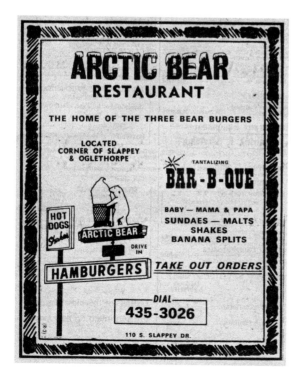

Albany's Arctic Bear Restaurant became famous as the site of a 1959 sit-in during the civil rights era, but even without that distinction, its polar bear/ice cream cone neon signage would have made it notable. Variations of it could be found atop scores of drive-ins throughout Georgia and many other states. After the eatery closed, the sign was preserved as a historical artifact.

At the Robin Hood Motel in Jonesboro, we have to assume they attempted to take from the rich (tourists, that is) and give to the poor (or at least the owners and their dependents). As with the Farm House seen earlier, it is amusing that the Robin Hood postcard describes its location five miles south of Atlanta's city limits as "a beautiful rustic setting." *Al Coleman collection.*

Hopefully, folks were as jolly as Robin Hood's Merrie Men after a night's stay at the Jolly Inn on I-75 at Valdosta. It might not have been as lavish as Valdosta's Pines Camp of forty years before, but it served its purpose for the newer breed of interstate traffic.

One would think that a park such as Six Flags Over Georgia would have spurred the development of a plethora of motels and restaurants in its neighborhood, but such was not the case—possibly because Six Flags was open for only approximately half the year, and such businesses had to make a profit year-round. The Matador Motor Inn had the advantage of being within walking distance of Six Flags' front gate, but even that was not enough to keep it from being gored by progress.

Comparison time again: The billboard for the Ashburn Motor Inn ("the Quiet One") featured the snoozing emblem of its Honeybear Restaurant. The Charlton Motel at Folkston was owned by the same family, only its billboards had a sleeping figure more reminiscent of the Okefenokee's most famous comic strip denizen, Pogo Possum. *Both, Al Coleman collection.*

What with Waycross being almost the last stop before U.S. I bravely flowed into Florida, it made sense that some motels would choose that semitropical theme. The Palms Court was one of those. This sign was there when the author's family stayed at the Palms in 1968 and was still shining brightly in 1992. However, in the intervening years, all traces of the motel have been eliminated.

With so many neon signs being short and to the point—MOTEL, EAT, NO VACANCY and so on—try to put yourself in the position of a sign maker tasked with spelling out the name of the Okefenokee Motel in Folkston. At least the establishment chose to have a nighttime image made for its postcards, showing the complex in all its colorful splendor.

Waycross's Green Frog Restaurant was a local landmark. It got its name not only from its proximity to the Okefenokee but also from its house specialty of fried frog legs. These two views from about twenty years apart show how the appearance of the building changed.

It is quite obvious how the Blue Top Tourist Court got its moniker. Another educated guess, not indicated on its postcards, is that at some point in its early life it was connected with the Pure Oil Company's identical cottage-shaped service stations.

The names selected for the innumerable mom-and-pop motels of the nation's highways could range from the mundane to the outlandish. Certainly, no one passing through Glennville on U.S. 301/25 could ignore the Cheeri-O Motel and its adjoining Glass House Restaurant. No, we don't know if Cheerios were on the breakfast menu.

OPPOSITE: The mom-and-pop motels became an endangered species as motel chains came into their own, although the two approaches managed to coexist for many years. In 1992, this rusting early billboard for the Holiday Inn at Albany could still be seen along U.S. 80, but not for much longer.

ABOVE: One of the first chains to take root in the pre-interstate days was Howard Johnson's, they of the orange roofs, fried clams and twenty-eight flavors of ice cream. By the early 1940s, Howard Johnson's restaurants could be found "from Maine to Florida," as the advertising put it. *Al Coleman collection.*

As if the restaurants were not common enough sights, Howard Johnson's really cemented its roadside presence when it began a chain of motels. This was the first Howard Johnson's Motor Lodge, staking its initial claim in Savannah in 1954.

Today, only nostalgic old-timers even remember when there were Howard Johnson's restaurants. The chain survives only as a brand name for low-budget motels. This former restaurant sits along U.S. 1 at Folkston and would have been the last one encountered before crossing into Florida. *Russell Wells collection.*

Another common chain was Ramada Inn, but not all of its locations were quite as lavish as this one in Valdosta. Note the early Ramada Inn logo featuring the trumpet-blowing, balding innkeeper known officially as Uncle Ben.

HAHIRA, GEORGIA

OPPOSITE, TOP: As U.S. I made its way toward Florida, a former Holiday Inn at Folkston was eventually folded into the Ramada Inn chain. By 1992, it was abandoned, and the subtropical foliage was about to turn the property into a Dixie jungle (no, wait, that was another attraction). Amazingly, the building survived and now serves as a rental storage facility.

OPPOSITE, BOTTOM: Dairy Queen has long been a roadside tradition, But how many people remember this 1960s trademark character, a little Dutch girl with a head and bonnet shaped like DQ's familiar logo? She was still perched on a weathervane atop an older style Dairy Queen in Rockmart in 2006.

ABOVE: Days Inn is still a familiar presence along the interstates, but not its companion chain of on-site restaurants known as Tasty World. Note the Days Inn sign with its logo indicating the room price of eight bucks per night. It was definitely a different era, and that is what this entire book has been intended to preserve. Pleasant dreams and pleasant travels!

Bibliography

Adkinson, Tom. "Krofft: It's Not Six Flags Under Glass." *Southern Living* (December 1976).

Cashin, Edward J. *The Story of Augusta*. Augusta, GA: Richmond County Board of Education, 1980.

Clemmons, Jeff. *Rich's: A Southern Institution*. Charleston, SC: The History Press, 2012.

Corson, Pete. "Exploring Atlanta's Lost Amusement Parks." *Atlanta Journal-Constitution*, May 17, 2016.

Erickson, Hal. *Sid and Marty Krofft: A Critical Study of Saturday Morning Children's Television, 1969–1993*. Jefferson, NC: McFarland and Company, 1998.

Freeman, David B. *Carved in Stone: The History of Stone Mountain*. Macon, GA: Mercer University Press, 1997.

Hollis, Tim. *Dixie Before Disney: 100 Years of Roadside Fun*. Jackson: University Press of Mississippi, 1999.

———. *Six Flags Over Georgia*. Charleston, SC: Arcadia Publishing, 2006.

———. *Stone Mountain Park*. Charleston, SC: Arcadia Publishing, 2009.

———. *Stuckey's*. Charleston, SC: Arcadia Publishing, 2017.

Jakle, John A., Keith A. Sculle and Jefferson S. Rogers. *The Motel in America*. Baltimore, MD: Johns Hopkins University Press, 1996.

King, Wayne. "Underground Atlanta Complex Is Beset by Problems." *New York Times*, February 19, 1975.

Onosko, Tim. *Fun Land U.S.A.* New York: Ballantine Books, 1978.

Poole, Shelia. "Last Year for First Baptist's Atlanta Passion Play." *Atlanta Journal-Constitution*, March 31, 2011.

Porter, Doug. "Memories of Tift Park Zoo Fading with Time." *Albany (GA) Herald*, May 25, 2019.

Pousner, Howard. "Cyclorama to Make Big Move to Atlanta History Center." *Atlanta Journal-Constitution*, July 23, 2014.

Roberts, Clifford. *The Story of the Augusta National Golf Club*. Garden City, NY: Doubleday, 1978.

Rose, Michael, Paul Crater and Don Rooney. *Lost Atlanta*. London: Pavilion Books, 2015.

Sammarco, Anthony Mitchell. *A History of Howard Johnson's*. Charleston, SC: The History Press, 2013.

About the Author

Tim Hollis has written thirty-four books on pop culture history, a number of them concerning southeastern tourism. He also operates his own museum of vintage toys, souvenirs and other pop-culture artifacts near Birmingham, Alabama.

Visit us at
www.historypress.com